Spirit of the Dragon

The Story of Jean Lumb

A Proud Chinese Canadian

林黃彩珍

by *Arlene Chan*

TrueValue Series

The Value of the Family

UMBRELLA PRESS

Toronto

Dedication: *To my family*

Publisher:	Ken Pearson
Design:	Ron & Ron Design & Photography
Calligraphy:	Ma Shiu-Yu
Cover Photograph:	Cavouk
Artist:	Bill Kimber
Illustration of the Dragon:	
Concept:	Frank Hsu
Designer:	Ian Leventhal

The Author and Publisher gratefully appreciate the kind assistance of all those who contributed to this publication.

Every reasonable effort has been made to trace ownership of copyright material. Information will be welcome which will enable the publisher to rectify any reference or credit in future printings.

Canadian Cataloguing in Publication Data
Chan, Arlene
      Spirit of the dragon : the story of Jean Lumb, a proud Chinese Canadian

(TrueValue series)
Includes bibliographical references and index.
ISBN 1-895642-31-0 (bound) ISBN 1-895642-24-8 (pbk)

1. Lumb, Jean. 2. Chinese Canadians - Biography. *
3. Women civic leaders - Canada - Biography. 4. Women social reformers - Canada - Biography. I. Title. II. Series.
FC106.C5Z7 1997   971.064′2′092   C97-930262-5   F1034.3.P74C53 1997

Three Panes and a Star / A *kennyp* Publication

Manufactured in Canada

UMBRELLA PRESS
56 Rivercourt Blvd.
Toronto, ON. M4J 3A4
Tel: (416) 696-6665
Fax: (416) 696-9189
E-mail: umbpress@interlog.com
www.interlog.com/~umpress

Introduction

The story of Jean Lumb is one among many that could be told about Chinese-Canadian women who were raised during the Great Depression and the Second World War. Despite the hardships of living in a Canada that did not welcome Chinese people, Jean grew and developed from being an "outsider" to being a leader not only within the Chinese-Canadian community but also in the whole of Canada.

Like the mighty dragon in Chinese mythology, her spirit and determination have made her a symbol to be admired by all people. Through her leadership, Jean Lumb is a woman who has made a difference to life in Canada.

At right, Jean Lumb's name written in Chinese characters .

Ferry Boat Tragedy

"Help me! Help me!" cried out the woman, her eyes filled with terror.

Just a moment earlier, she had been sitting quietly in the front seat on the lower deck of the ferry boat. Suddenly, there was a crash as the ferry was rammed by a larger ship, the *Princess Alice*. Now, she was pinned under the sharp bow of the *Princess Alice*.

"Help me! Help me!" Those were her last dying words.

"I'll never forget the screams of that woman," Jean Lumb says as she remembers the ferry boat tragedy of 1935. Fourteen-year-old Jean always sat in the same seat when she took the 7:30 A.M. ferry to work from Vancouver across the harbour to

North Vancouver. She never failed to be the first in line at the
dock for the ten-minute ride so that she could sit in the same
seat the lady had taken that day. Although Jean was paid only
two dollars a week for baby-sitting, her family relied on her
earnings, and she had to go to her job every day.

However, by chance, she was not first in line that day. A
woman, on her way to her grandson's birthday party, had
missed the earlier ferry and so she was at the head of the line
for the next one. She took the seat that Jean had always
occupied and Jean had to sit farther back on the ferry.

Jean recalls years later, "It was so foggy that morning. But
when I saw that big ship, I knew we were going to be hit." Jean
was thrown across the cabin with the impact of the crash.
Sensing great danger, she grabbed a fellow passenger who was

in a state of shock, climbed over the empty seats, and ran up the stairs to the main deck of the ferry. All the passengers were pulled to safety aboard the *Princess Alice* just in time. Seconds later, the ferry sank.

News of the accident spread quickly on the radio. When it was announced that a woman had been pinned by the collision and had drowned, Jean's mother thought the worst. She knew that Jean always sat in the lower deck at the front. To her relief, it was announced that the person who died was an older woman. Her mother then knew that it could not be Jean.

Jean's mother knew that her daughter was going to be someone special.

There is an old Chinese saying that if someone survives a disaster, that person will have good fortune.

Report of the accident, appearing in the newspaper:

Vancouver

On Monday, February 4, 1935, at 8·47 A.M., the worst fears became stark reality: *West Vancouver 5* was rammed and sunk by the CPR's *Princess Alice*.

"It is alleged," said the *West Vancouver News* on February 7, "the ferry was on her right course and going slowly. She was struck on the side of the large cabin aft, the sharp bow of the *Alice* striking at an acute angle and bringing up at the bulkhead on the side of the stairway. This allowed those in the cabin to escape up the stairway, but an elderly lady, believed to be Mrs. William E. Burritt, mother of Mrs. A. P. Croker, of 2869 Bellevue Avenue, was trapped between the bow of the *Alice* and the side of the cabin. Captain [Darius] Smith risked his life, as did Mate [George] Hayes and Lookout Arnold Garthone, who came to his assistance, in a gallant attempt to save her, the captain receiving a bad cut in the head, but the ferry sank before she could be extricated. The surviving passengers … were taken on the *Alice* to the city …

Growing Up in British Columbia

Jean Wong was born on July 30, 1919, in Nanaimo, a small town on Vancouver Island in British Columbia. Her father had come to Canada from China in 1899 to work as a farm labourer for a landowner named Mr. Billy. "With Mr. Billy's help," Jean

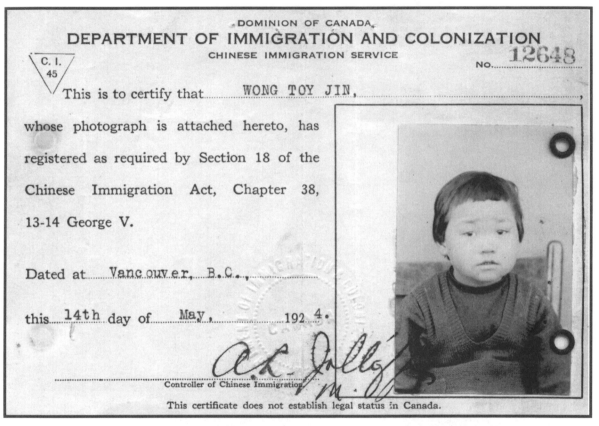

When the Exclusion Act was enacted in 1923, all Chinese living in Canada had to be registered. This certificate is Jean's registration – her name as a child was Wong Toy Jin.

explains, "my father was soon able to bring my mother and my eldest brother, who was six, from China to Canada." Later, her father left the farm and became a coal miner, again with the help of Mr. Billy. Eight more children, including Jean, were born to the family in Nanaimo. The family was very poor and struggled for a living, but no one complained. Her father knew that no matter how bad things were, life would have been worse if they still lived in China.

When the coal mine closed, the Wong family moved from Nanaimo to Vancouver, where Jean's father opened a fruit store and leased a hotel. It was now the early 1930s and there were no jobs for people. This period was called the Great Depression. With no money, people stopped travelling and staying in hotels. Instead, her father rented rooms to people who lived there and a few who stayed overnight on their journey back to China.

Jean recalls, "With almost a full house, few had enough money to pay and my father lost his hotel business. He could not pay the rent because he was not able to collect any money." The family moved out of the 100-room hotel into a small apartment and worked in the fruit store. Three more children were born, bringing the number of children to 12 – five sons and seven daughters.

At this time, there was discrimination against Chinese people as they were considered different. Their language was not English. Employers paid them lower wages than other people. They did not have the right to vote. They could not become professionals, such as lawyers, teachers or pharmacists. Their children had to attend segregated schools. That meant that white children did not go to the same school as the other children, including

Sister Wynnie (middle) *says farewell to Jean* (right) *and Dorothy* (left) *at the train station in Vancouver as they leave for Toronto.*

Native peoples, Chinese, and Japanese. To get to her school, Jean recalls, she had to walk past the school the white children attended. As she walked by, insults would be yelled at her.

At the age of 12, although she loved school, Jean had to quit to work in her father's fruit store to help support the family. In those days, there was no law about staying in school. Looking back, Jean says, "Father took me out of school to work so Robert, my older brother, could go on in school." She feels very proud of this sacrifice because her brother later graduated from university as an aeronautical engineer.

The night she had to leave school she cried. Her father came into her room and told her not to worry about leaving school. He would be her teacher. And so, with her older brother's school books, she studied during the evenings after working in the store all day.

Her father also taught her how to read and write Chinese. "I learned more Chinese from my father than I would have at

A model of the airplane Jean's brother, Robert, built and flew.

school," Jean remembers. Her father took her to work with him when he still ran the hotel. Every day, she had to copy names in the registration book to practice her Chinese. During this time, she became very close to her father, and his teaching was to influence her for the rest of her life.

The precious time with her father passed. One of her older sisters had married and moved to Toronto to open a fruit store. She wrote and asked her parents for help from the family. So at age 16 Jean found herself on the train from Vancouver to Toronto with her sister Dorothy, age 8, to work for her older married sister.

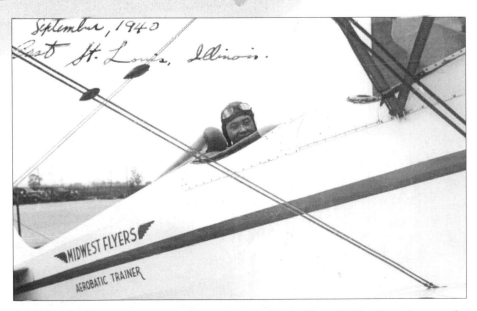

During the Second World War, Robert trained pilots. Following the war, he and his brother, Tommy, started Central Airways, a successful flying school on Toronto Island.

The Move to Toronto

For the train ride, Jean was given only some ham, a loaf of bread and one dollar to buy something to drink. Dorothy, her eight-year old sister, was with her. "One less mouth to feed," was her mother's reason for sending her along.

Jean at her fruit store, 1938.

Jean had mixed feelings. She was scared about having to look after her little sister. But, she was very excited about travelling for the first time and the adventure of starting a new life. The girls had to sit up all the way on hard, wooden seats. They could not afford a sleeping berth or even the section with cushioned seats. The excitement quickly wore off after travelling for four days and three nights.

Jean at her fruit store, 1938

"There were so few Chinese in Toronto at that time," she remembers, upon arriving in the city, "mostly lonely men, whose wives and children were far away in China."

Her sister's fruit store was not doing well so they all left Toronto to look for a new place to start a business. Finally, after much searching, they opened a restaurant in Sudbury, a mining town in Northern Ontario. After a year, Jean moved back to Toronto with Dorothy to work for a cousin who owned a fruit store in that city.

In those days, Chinese found it difficult to find work. So they opened restaurants, laundries or grocery stores. A short time later, with the help of relatives and a loan of $200, Jean opened her own fruit store at the age of 17. With very little money and education, but a great deal of experience working in fruit stores, she was able to start her own business.

Within a few years, Jean's business was doing well enough for her to bring her parents, brothers and sisters to Toronto. Little did Jean know that by moving her family there she would be preparing for the next big event of her life.

A New Life

Jean was now 19 years old, and the family thought that it was time for her to marry. At that time in the Chinese community, it

Jean and her husband, Doyle, with Jean's parents and sister, Frances, at their wedding. Jean lost her Canadian citizenship when she married someone who was not born in Canada. She later applied to regain her citizenship in 1957.

was the custom for the family to select someone, called a "matchmaker," to arrange a marriage between two young people. The matchmaker would match people with similar backgrounds and interests so that the marriage would have a good chance of lasting. With the help of a matchmaker, Jean was introduced to Doyle Lumb. "He was such a good looking

boy," she remembers, "and very quiet." Jean's mother thought it would be all right because "Jean talks a lot." One reason Doyle was selected by the matchmaker was that he owned a fruit store, just like Jean. The matchmaker thought Jean and Doyle would have many things in common.

"My mother asked me if I liked him. If I didn't like him, I didn't have to see him anymore." Jean did like Doyle, and she knew her mother liked him too. She married Doyle in 1939 at

"Jean was a wonderful hostess at the restaurant. She was so bubbly, alive and gracious – she was all those things. In those days, the Kwong Chow was the best Cantonese restaurant in Toronto."

Pierre Berton, author

the age of 20. Jean and Doyle were married for 50 years until he died in 1989.

Jean insisted on being married in a church, not a community hall like the Chinese brides before her. She and Doyle were the first Chinese in Toronto to be married in a church.

Jean and her husband worked together in their grocery store. During their 20 years there, they raised six children – three boys and three girls. Jean became a Christian, partly for her children. "I wanted them to have all the things I had missed, like Sunday School, Boy Scouts and Girl Guides."

Jean and Doyle decided to open a restaurant, rather than continue the grocery store. In 1959, they opened the restaurant in downtown Chinatown and called it Kwong Chow, named after a city in China – famous for its Cantonese cuisine. The restaurant was successful for many years and attracted well-known people over the years from prime ministers and politicians to movie stars and theatre people.

Even though Jean worked long hours, she knew how important it was to spend time with her husband and her children. She knew how important this was because her father had taught her the value of family life and relationships. "My father loved his family," recalls Jean. "Family was the most precious thing in the world." It was this sense of value for the family that led to a powerful change in Canadian law.

Celebrating VE Day to mark the end of the Second World War. Jean is third from the left, front row.

Meeting the Prime Minister

"What did he say?" asked the Prime Minister of Canada as he leaned towards Jean.

In 1957, over 20 Chinese Canadians chosen from across the country were in Ottawa to ask Prime Minister John Diefenbaker to change the immigration law that separated Chinese families.

Earlier there had been a tax, called a "Head Tax", on Chinese coming to Canada. Then in 1923, the government introduced the "Exclusion Act" to stop more Chinese from coming to Canada. For 24 years, no Chinese could come to Canada. The law kept families apart – husbands in Canada, wives and children in China. Even when the government ended the Exclusion Act in 1947, families continued to be separated. Only Chinese who were Canadian citizens could bring their families over to Canada. If someone wanted his mother to come, she had to be older than 65. Only children 18 years old or younger could come.

Exclusion Act, 1923

After the railroad was built across Canada, the Chinese workers were no longer needed. The government introduced a head tax of $10 in 1886 to discourage Chinese from coming to Canada. Over the next few years, it was raised to $50, $100 and then $500. Still, the Chinese kept coming to Canada. Finally, in 1923, the Exclusion Act was passed and that stopped the immigration from China to Canada and it lasted 24 years, until 1947. Jean's husband, Doyle, paid the $500 head tax when he came to Canada at the age of 12. He was one of the last Chinese to enter the country before the Exclusion Act of 1923.

This was unfair and kept families apart, and Jean, who valued family life, knew how unjust it was. Jean was invited to join the group that was to meet with the Prime Minister. The group travelled to Ottawa from across Canada to try to

persuade the Canadian government to change the law so that
families could be together.

*Jean at the meeting with Prime Minister John Diefenbaker in 1957. Mr. Wong
is seated on the other side of the prime minister.*

"What did he say?" Prime Minister Diefenbaker asked
again. He had asked Jean, the only woman delegate, to sit next
to him during the presentation. The leader, Mr. Wong, was
giving a speech to explain the reasons why the group thought
the law should be changed. Jean knew his speech by heart
because she had helped Mr. Wong, the official spokesperson, to
practice it over and over again on the train ride to Ottawa. Each
time the Prime Minister asked, she repeated what Mr. Wong
had said.

"You saved the day, Jean!" exclaimed Mr. Wong after the
meeting.

"The change to the immigration laws was my greatest
accomplishment," says Jean. She had carried out her father's
dream to see Chinese families re-united.

It was years later that Jean discovered that Prime Minister Diefenbaker had trouble hearing in one ear. Jean was sitting on the side of the Prime Minister's good ear, and Mr. Wong on the side of his bad ear. From that day, Jean became known as the unofficial spokesperson for the Chinese community.

Jean's passionate involvement with politics was a result of her father's influence. Earlier, in 1947, with the end of the Exclusion Act, Chinese Canadians were finally accepted as citizens with the right to vote. Proudly, Jean's father voted twice before his death. He knew the importance of voting and its effect on the community. He would have been very proud of Jean on that day as she sat beside the Prime Minister – and helped to change the law! Her strong feelings about the value of the family had helped change the law allowing Chinese and other people to bring their families together in Canada.

Exactly ten years later, Jean went back to Ottawa to meet another important person.

Prime Minister John Diefenbaker and his wife, Olive, at Jean's restaurant.

Meeting the Queen of England

Happy birthday! It was Canada's Centennial, its 100th anniversary as a country. A grand celebration was organized for June 30 and July 1, 1967, in Ottawa for Canadians and for Her Majesty, the Queen.

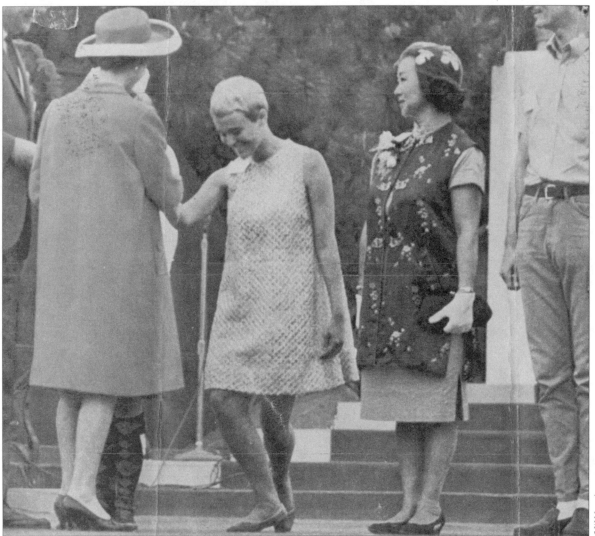

Jean waiting to be presented to Queen Elizabeth in Ottawa, 1967.

S W Magazine

The Chinese Community Dancers of Ontario, a dance group that Jean had formed, was chosen to perform for the celebration in Ottawa. "I can't go," was Jean's first reaction. "My son, Doug, is getting married that day." John Fisher, known as "Mr. Canada" because he wrote and told stories about the history of Canada, insisted, "Jean, you have to go. It's a command performance for the Queen!"

A private airplane was arranged for Jean and her three daughters. "In one day we were in Ottawa dancing for the show. I was presented to the Queen at 3 PM," she remembers. "Then we had to rush off to catch the plane to Toronto for Doug's wedding that evening at 7 PM. The next morning, we were back in Ottawa for the July 1st performance." Jean's mother, so proud of her daughter, told her, "The sky opened and let you into heaven."

Governor General Roland Michener at Jean's restaurant.

Community Work

Jean's work with the Chinese Community Dancers of Ontario was only one of the many ways that she volunteered her time in the Chinese community. She helped out at the public schools, Chinese school, and community centre that her children attended. She donated her time to the Lumb Family Association and to a Chinese drama group.

Bill Cosby sent Jean a signed photograph after meeting her and enjoying a meal at the restaurant.

In the late 1960s, Jean helped in a campaign to save Toronto's Chinatown. She was in charge of representatives from over 40 Chinese organizations who went to City Hall to save their Chinatown. Wealthy businessmen with their own ideas about improving the downtown area wanted to tear it down and build expensive high-rise apartments and offices. Jean and her group convinced the city politicians that Chinatown had to

Family Associations

Family Associations were very important to the Chinese. People with the same surname believed that they were descended from the same ancestor. These family associations helped their members, especially during hard times. Jean was a member of the Wong Association. After her marriage, she and Doyle were active in the Lem Si Ho Tong Family Association. (Her married name was Lumb – and Lumb and Lem are different spellings in English for the same surname).

be saved. It was important to the Chinese community and to the people of the city. Led by the mayor of Toronto, David Crombie, the city limited the height of new buildings to four

> *"I remember Jean as an energetic, hard-working, and kind person. She loved her family and made an enormous contribution to her community. She is one of Toronto's great heroes and I have always been proud to call her my friend."*
> *David Crombie, former Mayor of Toronto*

storeys. Chinatown was saved. Toronto's Chinatown was not alone in its fight against being demolished. Jean went to Vancouver and Calgary as the only woman representative to help save their Chinatowns too.

Another important event for Jean in the 1960s was meeting Pauline McGibbon, who later became the Lieutenant Governor

Jean and David Crombie, Mayor of Toronto, at the Kwong Chow restaurant, 1968.

Pauline McGibbon, former Lieutenant Governor of Ontario, influenced Jean to participate in the Arts and community work.

of Ontario, the Queen's official representative in the province. She encouraged Jean to extend her volunteer work outside the Chinese community and into the Canadian way of life. Taking Pauline McGibbon's advice, Jean worked as a volunteer in a number of organizations, including the Women's College Hospital, Summer Centres for Seniors, University Settlement House, and Mount Sinai Hospital.

To do volunteer activity outside the Chinese community was a huge step to take for a Chinese Canadian, particularly a woman. It had been the custom for Chinese, like many other immigrant groups, to stay within their own community. For someone to work outside it was a remarkable achievement. But then, Jean was a remarkable woman.

Jean became the interpreter of Chinese thoughts, feelings, and needs for non-Chinese people and for all levels of government. She was constantly interviewed by newspapers, magazines, radio, and television for her opinions. She provided an important link between Chinese Canadians and the community outside Chinatown.

Jean's work in the Chinese community was so important that she returned to Ottawa to become the first Chinese-Canadian woman to receive Canada's highest honour given to its citizens.

"Jean was like a Mayor of Chinatown. It was easy to understand. She was so outgoing and interested in the community and Chinatown. She played an outstanding role in Toronto's history."

Ed Mirvish, owner of restaurants and theatres

The Order of Canada

Jean's knees were shaking. Everyone was looking at her. She was in Ottawa to receive the Order of Canada. "What are they going to say about me?" Jean wondered. Along with Jean, many famous Canadians were honoured, including James Reaney, the poet and playwright; William Kurelek, the painter; and Jack Bush, the painter.

Jean receiving the Order of Canada from Governor General Jules Léger in Ottawa, 1976. Her first thought when told of her award: "What am I going to wear?"

At the presentation of the Order of Canada, Jean remembers hearing how she was a defender of Chinatown. She also heard that she was the only woman representing the Chinese community in the appeal to change the immigration laws. The change allowed for the re-unification of families that had been separated by Canada's Exclusion Act of 1923.

Jean was naturally full of emotion when she received the Order of Canada. "I cried and so did Doyle. We were thinking of all the others who had worked so hard for the causes of our people too," remembers Jean. She also cried for her mother and father who did not live long enough to see their daughter so honoured.

Jean and Doyle at the Order of Canada ceremony.

Continuing Recognition

Jean has received many awards and honours since she was awarded the Order of Canada. One year later, she returned to

Hal Jackman, Lieutenant Governor of Ontario, honouring Jean at the "Jean Lumb Awards of Excellence," 1996.

Ottawa again to be honoured for her community work. She received the Queen's Silver Jubilee Award, presented by the Queen, on the occasion of Her Majesty's 25 years of rule. The Right Honourable Jules Léger presented her with the Governor General's Award on the same day.

In 1982, Jean was the first woman to receive the Fran Deck Award, given to the person who makes an important contribution to Toronto's restaurant industry. "This was a really special award," remembers Jean. "All the years of hard work at the Kwong Chow restaurant were recognized. It was the first time a Chinese restaurant had won the award too!"

In 1983, Jean was honoured at the 125th anniversary celebration of the Chinese community in Canada for being an outstanding Chinese Canadian.

"I love Jean. She's a kind, generous and beautiful lady, a very special person with unbelievable strength of character. Goodness shines from her face."

Ann Mirvish, actress and artist

In 1984, Jean won the Award of Merit, Toronto's top honour. "What a year to win," recalls Jean, "It was the same year as Toronto's 150th birthday."

Jean now serves as a Citizenship Judge representing Canada when immigrants are sworn in as Canadian citizens. She continues her community work with the Mount Sinai Hospital, Yee Hong Nursing Home for Greater Toronto and the Chinese Cultural Centre of Greater Toronto.

In honour of her great accomplishments, the Jean Lumb Awards of Excellence are awarded every year to outstanding students of Chinese-Canadian descent from schools in the city of Toronto.

Throughout her life, Jean has lived by the values her parents taught – values held dear by generations of Chinese – and many other people around the world. These include the importance of family life, obedience, respect for elders, and education.

As she said so well herself at the Dragon Ball in 1990, honouring her accomplishments – speaking to an audience of over 1,200 people –

Jean as Citizenship Judge with Metro Toronto Police Chief David Boothby.

"Through the hard work and sacrifices of our forefathers, they have passed on a legacy of loyalty, honour, obedience, and respect. Through education, through the strength of family unity, and through respect for one another, we, the Chinese Canadians, have inherited a broad and firm foundation as good responsible citizens. I am proud, I am very happy, to be a Canadian."

Sitting in her home, the walls covered with family pictures, Jean recalls, "The most important thing that my father left with me was his love for people, especially family. He used to say to me, 'Jean, no matter what happens, always go to your family first. Your family is the most important thing. You may have friends, you may have people with other interests, but you'll find that it is your family that counts.'"

Even though the importance of family is a strong Chinese tradition, Jean believes that it does not matter about one's background. To her, "a family is a family". During all her years of community work, she remembers, "If I didn't have the family behind me, I really couldn't have done it. Because if your family isn't with you, beside you always , you really can't do anything. And if your family is strong, this will make our country strong too!"

Jean lives in Toronto where her children and nine grandchildren are "my life and my joy". Her mother was right: Jean feels blessed with her good fortune.

Jean's Accomplishments

President, Women's Association of Ontario

Founder, Chinese Restaurant Association of Ontario

Founder, Chinese Business Association of Ontario

Director, Women's Association of the Chinese Dramatic Society

Trustee, Toronto Chinese Public School

President, Lem Si Ho Tong Family Association Women's Group

Member, Ontario Advisory Council on Multiculturalism

First Chinese-Canadian woman appointed to:
Board of Governors, Women's College Hospital
Board member, Rotary Laughlen Centre
Board of Directors, University Settlement House

Director, Mount Sinai Hospital

Director, Summer Centres for Seniors

Honourary Member, Ontario Women's Directorate

Citizenship Court Judge

Founding Director, Yee Hong Nursing Home for Greater Toronto

Honourary Advisor, Chinese Cultural Centre of Greater Toronto

Jean's Awards

Order of Canada, 1976

Queen's Silver Jubilee Medal, 1977

Governor General's Award, 1977

Fran Deck Award to recognize Toronto's leading contributor to the restaurant industry, 1982

Special Award to Honour Special Chinese Canadians, 1983

City of Toronto Award of Merit, 1984

Ontario Chinese Restaurant Association Award, 1984

YWCA Women of Change Honour Roll, 1984

Award, Ontario Women's Directorate, 1993

Toronto and Area Council of Women, 100th Anniversary Award, 1993

Jean Lumb Awards of Excellence, 1996

For More Information About Jean Lumb

Chinese Canadian National Council. The Women's Book Committee. *Jin Guo: Voices of Chinese Canadian Women.* Toronto: Toronto Women's Press, 1992.

Huang, Evelyn with Lawrence Jeffrey. *Voices from a Community.* Vancouver: Douglas & McIntyre, 1992.

"Quo Vadis, Mrs.Lumb." National Film Board, [196-].

Yee, Paul, *Struggle and Hope: The Story of Chinese Canadians.* Toronto: Umbrella Press, 1996.

For More Information About the Chinese in Canada

Canada. Multiculturalism Directorate. *The Canadian Family Tree.* Supply & Services Canada, 1979.

Harris, Heather and Mary Sun. *The Chinese Canadians.* Toronto: Nelson Canada, 1982.

Hoe, Ban Seng. *Beyond the Golden Mountain: Chinese Cultural Traditions in Canada.* Ottawa: Canadian Museum of Civilization, 1989.

Lee, Wai-man. *Portraits of Challenge: An Illustrated History of the Chinese Canadians.* Toronto: Council of Chinese Canadians in Ontario, 1984.

Yee, Paul. *Struggle and Hope: The Story of Chinese Canadians.* Toronto: Umbrella Press, 1996.

Yee, Paul. *Tales from Gold Mountain: Stories of the Chinese in the New World.* Vancouver: Douglas & McIntyre, 1989.

Wright, Richard Thomas. *In a Strange Land: A Pictorial Record of the Chinese in Canada, 1788-1923.* Saskatoon: Western Producer Prairie Books, 1988.

Index

Berton, Pierre, 15
Billy, Mr., 8

Chinatown, 22-23
Chinese Community Dancers of Ontario, 21, 22
Chinese Exclusion Act, *see* Exclusion Act
Cosby, Bill, *photo.* 22
Crombie, David, Mayor of Toronto, 23; *photo.,* 23

Diefenbaker, John, Prime Minister, 17-18; *photo.,* 18, 19
discrimination, 9
Dragon Ball, 29

Exclusion Act, 8, 17-19

Family Associations, 22
ferry boat accident, 4-7
fruit store, 9,10,13,15; *photo.,* 12, 13

Great Depression, 9

Head Tax, 17
hotel, 9

Jackman, Hal, Lieutenant Governor, Ontario, *photo.,* 28

Kwong Chow Restaurant, 15

Léger, Jules, Governor General, 28; *photo.* 26
Lumb, Doyle, 14-15; *photo.* 14, 27

marriage, 14-15; *photo.,* 14
matchmaker, 14-15
McGibbon, Pauline, Lieutenant Governor, Ontario, 23-24; *photo.* 24
Mirvish, Ann, 28
Mirvish, Ed, *photo.* 25
Michener, Roland, Governor General, *photo.* 21

Order of Canada, 26-27; *photo.* 26, 27

Queen Elizabeth II, 20-21, 28; *photo.* 20

school, 9-11

train ride, 11-13

VE Day Parade, *photo.* 16

Wong, Dorothy, 11-12; *photo.* 9
Wong, Robert, 10
   airplane, *photo.* 10, 11
Wong, Tommy, 11

Jean with her family.